MODERNOSTALGIA

ROCKPORT

MODERNOSTALGIA

Mixing Personal Treasures and Modern Style

GLOUCESTER MASSACHUSETTS

ROCKPORT PUBLISHERS

Anna Kasabian / Nora Richter Greer

First published in the United States of America by
Rockport Publishers, Inc.
33 Commercial Street
Gloucester, Massachusetts 01930-5089
Telephone: (978) 282-9590
Facsimile: (978) 283-2742
www.rockpub.com

ISBN 1-56496-810-3
10 9 8 7 6 5 4 3 2 1

Cover Image: © Red Cover/Andreas von Einsiedel
Design: Stoltze Design
Layout and Production: *tabula rasa* graphic design

Printed in China

MODERNOSTALGIA

CONTENTS

introduction

It seems that our dawning millennium has thrown the Jetsons out of orbit. Few modern, "space-age" families lounge on shiny metal chairs or invest in disposable furniture. We still want our familiar classics—graceful Windsor dining chairs and beautiful French tables. But at the same time, we may be disappointed that our interiors aren't more stylish and contemporary—perhaps even more airy and clutter-free. We harken back to the Modernists who streamlined design at the beginning of the industrial era.

While living in unconventional times, we can't deny our dual interests in contemporary and traditional design. But no longer must we choose one style for our interiors, because we can harmoniously mix our heirloom pieces with contemporary design ideas. Although there aren't any rules, there are some goals, and *Modern Nostalgia* will describe and demonstrate these.

In the early 1900s, the architectural profession reacted against the excessive decoration of earlier styles, and modernism began. Because the machine age sought to create streamlined, practical, and efficient architecture, modernism brought a radical change to the materials, room layout, and furnishings of home design. These changes continued to evolve throughout the 20th century. While the decorative arts are flourishing once again, modernism still influences contemporary design.

Those who aren't interior designers may rarely see many examples of this "new style." So, what exactly do we mean by Modern Nostalgia? It could be described as the fusion of contemporary and traditional design—a weaving together of old and new.

This book examines various ways to blend contemporary and traditional throughout the home and demonstrates numerous helpful techniques. Perhaps the first task will be to clear our rooms of clutter so that our crowded rooms have new breathing space, atmosphere, and depth. Paring down to essentials will help to balance old and new elements and, in the process, we'll be creating a personal style that better states who we are and what is important to us. *Modern Nostalgia* is designed to help you accomplish all this.

TRADITIONAL ARCHITECTURAL FEATURES CAN COMPLEMENT VIRTUALLY ANY INTERIOR. PLACING SPARE OR CONTEMPORARY FURNISHINGS IN ROOMS WITH CLASSICAL MOLDINGS AND PANELING MAY JUST CREATE YOUR IDEAL ENVIRONMENT.

MODERN**ELEMENTS**

Our love affair with modern style began years ago, surfacing well before pop art and refusing to leave—even when our high-styled furnishings became less comfortable. As sleek loft apartments, minimalist office spaces, and chic suburban homes held sway, it became gauche to display quirky collections or beloved antiques. The purity and simplicity of clean, modern rooms created a wonderful sense of refuge and peace, yet a strict adherence to this minimalist lifestyle left many of us wondering if we had traded too much "life" for "style."

Modern Nostalgia proposes to help you find your own contemporary design style without sacrificing your beloved treasures. Whether it's a Victorian chaise lounge or an heirloom dining set, you'll learn to incorporate them into your contemporary home, retaining the most up-to-date look without surrendering your links to the past.

On the following pages are the formulas for creating modern spaces with ease and grace and simple approaches to incorporating the beauty and perfection of older objects. The rooms presented here are simple, clean, and modern—but all have the flexibility to welcome a few pieces with personal history. We challenge you to start afresh, with the concepts of placement, mood, proportion, and color clearly in mind. The goal is to streamline your living space—edit out all the unnecessary objects you live with—and then create your ideal contemporary environment that incorporates special touches from the past.

placement · mood · proportion · color

In a traditional room full of architectural detail, a simple wooden dining table pairs comfortably with sleek black chairs of contemporary texture and line.

placement

In any interior, the pleasing fusion between old and new pieces can generate a great feeling of atmosphere and depth, but if done carelessly it can cause an unnatural and disastrous look that interrupts the visual flow. The great secret here is in the placement. Making an attractive room is all about properly dividing its space to create various views and focal points from every vantage point. Careful placement of furnishings and collections will create focal points that enchant the viewer and direct attention where you want it to go. Even the smallest room should have at least one highlight—preferably, one that is exciting and unusual.

Another secret to blending old and new elements? Repetition. Even in the most unlikely surroundings, several copies of one great piece can reinforce its validity. Repetition also creates a sense of order—so that even if the actual styles of your furnishings and accents are wildly opposed, repetition will balance the mix.

THE TEXTURE OF A BELOVED CANE SETTEE IS REPEATED IN THE WICKER CHAIR AND CARPET TO UNIFY THIS CONTEMPORARY LIVING ROOM. NOTICE THE ECHOED LINES OF THE SETTEE IN THE BED GLIMPSED IN THE ADJACENT ROOM.

AN ARTISTIC SCALE MODEL OF A CHURCH
PROVIDES A FOCAL POINT AND LENDS
AN AIR OF SERENITY TO THIS SPARELY
APPOINTED BEDROOM. THE COLORS,
TEXTURES, AND FORMS OF THE FEW ELE-
MENTS IN THE ROOM WORK TOGETHER
TO CREATE THE PEACEFUL SETTING.

Develop the focal point of your room. Perhaps that modern painting in your living room or bedroom is the crown jewel of that space. Try designing the rest of the room as a contemporary composition around it, and carefully decide where you'll place each object. Use the lines of the sofa, chairs, tables, or bed to form an abstract, three-dimensional sculpture. Keep the components of your room spacious and airy, and let each arrangement have its own importance in relationship to the whole. Add your touch of the traditional and then step back and view the room from the side and from above. If you find this type of interior too museum-like, you can try the concept in a microcosm on a tabletop. Group objects that contrast in color, shape, size, and texture to create a dynamic focal point and display your collectibles in a unique way. Or use mirrors to create the optical illusion of depth in a small or unusual-sized room.

CONSIDER USING ART AS THE FOCAL POINT OF YOUR ROOM. HERE, NEUTRAL FURNISHINGS AND TEXTURAL ACCESSORIES PROVIDE EFFECTIVE COUNTERPOINT TO THE VIBRANT COLORS OF ANDY WARHOL PRINTS.

NOTICE HOW THE PLACEMENT OF FURNI-
TURE IN A NONDESCRIPT ROOM CAN
LEND SCULPTURAL COMPLEXITY TO THE
DESIGN. AS SHOWN, YOU CAN USE MIR-
RORS—OF CONTEMPORARY OR ANTIQUE
VINTAGE—TO ADD DEPTH TO ANY ROOM.
NOTICE HOW THE UNUSUAL STAIRCASE
DIVIDES THE LIVING SPACE INTO TWO
AREAS AND CREATES FURTHER DIMENSION.

BY CAREFULLY PLACING OBJECTS ON A
TABLE, YOU BECOME THE ARTIST. THIS
COMPOSITION COMBINES CHEERFUL
COLORS WITH SERENE NEUTRALS AND
SETS OFF SOFT ROSE PETALS WITH THE
TEXTURES OF CHINA AND WOOD. REFLEC-
TIONS IN THE GLASS SCREEN BEHIND
THE TABLE ADD SUBTLE SPARKLE.

Yes, we seek harmony in our interiors, but a totally harmonious room can be monotonous. A bit of variety and contrast is welcome. While in the past it was unspeakable to mix furniture styles, it is now more fashionable to mix and match. There is, however, an art to the comfortable contrast. Rhythm should be evident in the colors, textures, or shapes—and it helps to carry this rhythm from one room to another. For example, if you like traditional English design, go for the traditional bedroom. But to establish rhythm, hint at its style with an antique cabinet in the hallway. If you like Oriental design, introduce silks to the bedroom and teak in the dining room. Your grandfather's portrait may still hang in the foyer, though it contrasts with your contemporary living room. To create even rhythm without boredom, place new or old objects symmetrically around a fireplace or sofa, but not necessarily identical ones.

CONSIDER COUNTERBALANCING FORM AND COLOR AND ADDING UNEXPECTED ELEMENTS TO YOUR DESIGN. HERE, A MASSIVE GRAND PIANO IS SOFTENED BY A DELICATE METAL LATTICE CHAIR, AND THE PIANO IS PAINTED AN UNEXPECTED WHITE. A BOLD BLOCK OF ORANGE ON THE WALL BALANCES THE VISUAL WEIGHT OF THE PIANO, AND THE SLIGHT, CONTEMPORARY LIGHT FIXTURE MATCHES THE DELICATE OUTLINE OF THE CHAIR.

TRY TO ESTABLISH A VISUAL RHYTHM IN THE PLACEMENT OF OBJECTS. ABSOLUTE SYMMETRY CAN BE BORING, BUT AN ASYMMETRICAL ARRANGEMENT THAT IS WELL-BALANCED CAN BE HARMONIOUS AND COMFORTING.

Pare the room to its essentials, and
neatly tuck everything else away in
built-in bookshelves. Create comfortable contrasts, such as an everyday wooden table and chairs set by a
piece with unusual style.

mood

A space that is deliberately defined sets a mood, and an interior design will work best if you're able to define just the right atmosphere—cozy, sophisticated, suave, exotic, or contemporary with a touch of French traditional. So, when planning a contemporary room with nostalgic accents, first focus on that mood you want to create. Otherwise, you may be tempted to add furnishings, colors, or textures that work against it. You can easily absorb several traditional pieces or collections of nostalgic objects without making the room feel old fashioned. Mood can be established through the choice of furniture style, but also the upholstery and objects you choose. Think of a typical contemporary living room. Add a sofa covered in silk versus one covered in leopard skin. Quite a contrast in mood! Again, placement is crucial, as is the proportion and size of the furniture. Keep the modern goal of uncluttered space in mind. A distinctive atmosphere may, to some extent, dictate the way in which a room is used; take care that each element complements the room's purpose.

Even a spacious room with formal detailing can gain an air of warmth and intimacy when furnished with casual seating and warm, natural wood flooring and accents. The bare floor and open space keep the overall look clean and new.

A MODERN STRUCTURE TAKES ON
COTTAGE WARMTH—DELICATE WHITE
WICKER CHAIRS AND A COLORFUL
WOVEN RUG INVITE PASSERSBY TO SIT
AND RELAX FOR A WHILE.

Some pieces are inherently exotic—artifacts from foreign or ancient cultures spring to mind. With attention to its color and texture, proportion, form, and position in the room, you can incorporate an exotic piece into your contemporary décor, creating a happy fusion of cultures and styles. Repeat one of its features judiciously throughout the room to blend it with other objects without detracting from its importance. For example, incorporate a vibrant cloisonné vase into a neutral room by echoing a color in the vase in a throw pillow or small lampshade. Or, you may choose to repeat the form rather than the color of a piece. An embroidered, silk kimono hung as wall art can blend into a room with curvilinear furnishings if its angular lines are repeated, for example, in a coffee table or floor lamp. Even the unconventional use of an everyday object can lend a sense of the exotic to a room.

GLASS IS SHOWN TO BEST ADVANTAGE WHEN THERE'S ENOUGH SURROUNDING SPACE TO REFLECT ITS TRANSLUCENCE OR TRANSPARENCY.

SOMETIMES A PIECE IS SO EXOTIC THAT IT WORKS BEST ALONE. AN OLD BARBER'S CHAIR OF STRIKING COLOR, TEXTURE, AND FORM, WORKS WELL IN THIS CONTEMPORARY LIVING ROOM.

MIX THINGS UP INVENTIVELY. HERE,
THE RED OF THE QUIRKY CHANDELIER IS
REPEATED IN THE CHAIR CUSHIONS AND
ARTWORK. A STONE WALL AND A RUSTIC
TABLE BALANCE THIS CHIC ROOM FOR A
LOOK OF MODERN INFORMALITY.

Mood can be established through color, texture, or the inclusion of a specific object in your design. Another way to create mood, and to be able to change it whenever you please, is through the room's lighting. When glowing with the embers of fireplace logs, your living room has a much different atmosphere than when lit by an overhead fixture. Switching from incandescent to fluorescent lamps also can change a room's colors—and its mood—dramatically. Brilliant daylight pouring through uncovered windows gives any space a cheerful atmosphere.

It's important to consider lighting early in your design plans. Do you want only floor and table lamps, or do you want to install contemporary down lights or uplights? Just as lighting draws attention to actors on a stage, it should highlight and flatter a room's best features. The proper lighting can make or break a room, so also make sure that the natural and artificial light work well together.

COLOR CAN ALSO CREATE MOOD. HERE, A DINING TABLE COVERED IN WHITE LINEN IS ACCOMPANIED BY WHITE FRENCH CHAIRS AND A MATCHING SOFA IN GRAY AND WHITE UPHOLSTERY. TOGETHER, THEY CREATE A SOFT, RELAXED, YET ELEGANT SETTING IN A COZY ATTIC ROOM.

Natural textures of wood and wool
moderate the mood of sleek stainless steel, making this modern
kitchen as much a family gathering
place as it is the cook's laboratory.

proportion

The rooms in our house need balance just as our lives do. We often arrange our furniture to be complementary in size and shape, color and texture. It's obvious that a large, bulky sofa will dwarf a delicate, spindle-legged table. It is difficult to know what to do if your furnishings vary widely in scale. How do you add your bulky traditional pieces with sleek contemporary ones and still achieve balance? Try grouping smaller pieces together to counterbalance one larger piece. For example, by flanking a table with two chairs or hanging pictures alongside it, the eye is drawn upward and outward. This way, the table is perceived to be larger than it is, and it can counterbalance the massive sofa across the room. Think, again, of your space in three-dimensional terms and use the dimensions of height, depth, and width to achieve proportional balance. Decorative objects, such as large vases or ornamental grasses in vases, can be easily used to counterbalance larger objects. Allow the larger objects enough room to breathe and give the smaller ones good company to not seem isolated.

YOU CAN MIX AND MATCH TO YOUR HEART'S CONTENT IF YOU KEEP THE PRINCIPLES OF PROPORTION IN MIND. IN THIS CONTEMPORARY LIVING ROOM, A LARGE WOODEN VASE OFFSETS THE MASS OF THE STONE SHELL FOSSIL. NOTICE THAT BOTH OF THESE OBJECTS EXIST COMFORTABLY WITH THE CARVED FIREPLACE, PARTICULARLY AS OTHER EXOTIC PIECES ARE VISIBLE IN THE NEXT ROOM.

THE SYMMETRY IS QUITE RIGOROUS IN
THIS LIVING ROOM FILLED WITH DECORA-
TIVE ELEMENTS. EXPERIMENT WITH PRO-
PORTION TO SEE WHAT COMBINATIONS
WORK FOR YOU.

Modern Nostalgia allows for the mixture of contemporary and traditional styles, so don't be afraid to pair your square-backed dining room chairs with rounded-back ones. Or place a round side table in the same room with a larger square one. Mixing old, treasured pieces with contemporary furniture can make a difficult challenge easier if you consider scale and proportion, and particularly size comparisons. For example, if your contemporary and antique chairs are of the same height, they may look better together than if they were of nearly the same height and bulk. If placed near each other or at opposite ends of a room, these chairs will provide a balance to that space. On the other hand, a dramatic contrast can also be visually exciting. When playing with contrasts, however, you should establish an underlying rhythm—some repetition of form or size, or even color and texture, so that a sense of overall coherence is established. Use color and texture to bring more life to smaller pieces.

CREATE CONTRAST BY SETTING DARK OBJECTS AGAINST LIGHT ONES. HERE, THIS BLACK LACQUERED TABLE CREATES A STRONG SILHOUETTE AGAINST THE WHITE, PANELED WALL. ITS HEIGHT IS BALANCED BY A MODERN LAMP, WHICH IN TURN IS COUNTERBALANCED BY A SET OF WOODEN BOWLS.

EXPLORE THE UNUSED SPACE IN YOUR
ENTRYWAYS AND HALLWAYS. THESE MAY
OFFER SPECIAL OPPORTUNITIES FOR DIS-
PLAYING PIECES OF FURNITURE OR ART,
SUCH AS THIS TALL ANTIQUE CHEST OF
DRAWERS AND THE MODERN SIDE TABLE.

color

Color is a vital part of your design, and Modern Nostalgia leans toward light-colored interiors. Using an all-white palette in a room is an instant way to make everything appear more sleek and modern, and light and airy. Yet, bold colors can also enhance a contemporary space. The objective is to use blocks of colors, rather than a more detailed, decorative palette, to bring continuity to a room. Remember that bold colors can drastically change the proportions of your room, so before you paint, experiment with color samples. Large pieces of fabric or even flower arrangements can hint at how the new color scheme will look. Your palette choices can also be used as a means to create a visual flow between rooms. Or use a limited area of a darker wall color to visually change the dimensions of a room—to draw the eye to a certain section or provide a dramatic backdrop that highlights a particular piece of furniture.

THROW A MULTICOLORED RUG ON THE FLOOR TO COORDINATE UNMATCHED CHAIRS OF DIFFERENT COLORS.

A WELL-COORDINATED COLOR SCHEME,
SUCH AS THIS BOLD MIX OF IVORY,
YELLOW, TAN, AND GREEN, HELPS TO
UNIFY CONTEMPORARY AND TRADITIONAL
FURNISHINGS.

Don't be afraid of color, but use it judiciously. Color can balance or counterbalance a piece or furniture or a strong architectural feature, such as a large cupboard or a bank of windows. Color also can connect the diverse elements of a room. For example, you can repeat the natural color of wood in the rug or in a throw pillow or link several colors with a multicolored sofa fabric or wall hanging. You also can use color to highlight a special object or objects in a room, such as a striking collection of blue vases or plates. Or add a bit of the exotic through the texture of pillows, upholstery, curtains, or rugs, while maintaining a sleek appearance.

It's true that all things Oriental fascinated the Modernists. While Japanese and Chinese prints and rugs may no longer seem as exotic, they may help you create an atmosphere that is at once sophisticated, comforting, and unique. Keep the overall look—and the colors—simple and harmonious, and you can't go wrong.

THIS MONOCHROMATIC WHITE COLOR
SCHEME IS PARTICULARLY ELEGANT.
NOTICE HOW TEXTURE IS USED TO
SUBTLY ENHANCE THE DESIGN.

PAINT A DISTANT WALL A BOLD COLOR
TO DRAW THE EYE AND VISUALLY EXTEND
THE ROOM. CONTRASTING COLORS
ENLIVEN A ROOM'S INTERIOR.

MODERN**MIXES**

You've just been reminded of the modern idiom "less is more," and as you survey the rooms of your home, the sleek, spacious, and clutter-free interiors of *Modern Nostalgia* appeal to you. Yet, wholesale redecorating may not be a realistic option for financial and emotional reasons. How can you give up that nineteenth-century cabinet that your great-grandmother left you? Or that carved Chinese teak table found on your trip to the Far East? You may have incorporated several elements of contemporary design into your home, but how do you clear room space without losing a sense of individuality or personal history? In other words, how do you update a room without making it too contemporary?

First, relax and let yourself embrace the ideals of modern design. As mentioned, Modernism began in the early 1900s as a reaction against excessive decoration. It leans toward light, airy, and adaptable objects and emphasizes form, proportion, line, and texture. Again, a modern interior can be spoiled with too much furniture or too many objects.

You may find that its furnishings are made of materials introduced by the industrial revolution: tubular, chrome-plated metal; black Bakelite; stainless steel; large, unframed pieces of glass, plastics, and plywoods; polyesters; and curved and molded furniture.

In fact, with the machine age, the home was considered a streamlined machine for living. Each piece of furniture, each decorative object, and each painting was viewed as an essential part of a room for practical or aesthetic purposes. The remaining space was free from clutter and decorative embellishment, and white was the basic backdrop.

In the twenty-first century, these modern ideals are again being embraced, with a twist, as we search for a new level of comfort, for much has intervened between then and now. Creative designers are fusing the modern with the treasured old styles, bringing balance and harmony to personal décor. There is no right way to arrange a room, but the ultimate goal is an interior that expresses an overall coherence of form, color, and texture—a visual flow that is uninterrupted by clutter or dissonance. Each room in the public/private sanctuary that we call home must become a place for entertainment, relaxation, and enjoyment.

living · working · sleeping · bathing

BRING TOGETHER CONTEMPORARY AND
TRADITIONAL FURNISHINGS WITH EASE
AND CONFIDENCE, AS SEEN HERE IN A
FILLED, BUT NOT CROWDED, LIVING
ROOM. THE LARGE WINDOW PROVIDES AN
ABUNDANCE OF NATURAL LIGHT, GIVING
THE ROOM AN AIRY FEELING, AS DOES
THE HIGH CEILING.

living spaces

The process of blending time-honored objects into a modern setting is a simple one, and it can be the same for each room. First, clear the room (either in reality or in your mind) and study its basic architectural details. Elements such as bay windows, fireplaces, arches, and built-in bookshelves will obviously influence the interior design and are fixed, unless you plan to remodel. You will need to shape the interior furnishings and details around the architecture.

Keeping the room's function in mind, build your design around the most important objects—for example, the contemporary sofa, the antique chest, the patterned or textured rug, or your prized collection of nineteenth-century Chinese vases. Remember that a room often can be divided into two or more distinct areas, but be sure that there is continuity between the spaces. Experiment with placement, and punctuate your contemporary setting with traditional pieces. Work hard to keep the space as clutter free as possible, concentrating on the essentials as much as possible. Call upon your artistic impulses, even when arranging the books in your bookshelves. Keep examining every element you add, layer upon layer. In the end, you will discover a modern living space with a touch of your personality, which is extremely livable.

NOTICE HOW CONTEMPORARY CHAIRS DRESS UP THIS UNPRETENTIOUS ANTIQUE TABLE. IN THE BACKGROUND, CLEAN, CRISP BUILT-IN CABINETS DISPLAY A VARIED COLLECTION OF VASES AND CHINA.

CONSIDER THE STOVETOP AS AN INTEGRAL
PART OF YOUR WOODEN COUNTER TOP.
ITS SLEEK, STEEL FINISH IS ECHOED IN
UNDERSTATED SILVER CABINET PULLS.
ABOVE THE COUNTER, THE DISPLAY
BECOMES COLORFUL AND EXUBERANT.

defining living spaces

Our use of the living space in our homes is as varied and disparate as each individual and household. Yet even in the most formal living rooms, comfort is the overriding concern. And, in the case of modern nostalgia, this includes visual comfort—flowing, clutter-free spaces in which textures and colors blend to create pleasing vistas.

To get the most satisfaction from an interior design, first analyze how the room is used (for entertainment, relaxation, eating, reading, and so on) throughout each day. Obviously, the design of a formal living room will differ from that of the family room, since they will serve different purposes. Those of us fortunate enough to have more than an urban apartment's worth of square footage will identify with several of the living spaces mentioned on the following pages. Some of us need to be even more creative and design flexible spaces that can function both as formal and informal spaces.

USE ONE, DOMINANT PIECE TO BRING ALL YOUR EXOTICS TOGETHER, SUCH AS THE BLACK TRUNK USED HERE AS A COFFEE TABLE. THE EASY CHAIRS SET NEAR THE FIREPLACE CREATE A SENSE OF INTIMACY.

Don't be afraid to mix old pieces with new ones. As you can see, French Provincial chairs are successful at this very modern table. Repetition of curved and angular lines unifies the room.

family rooms

The family room, or all-purpose, free-flowing interior, is the most contemporary living space. Today's house design generally revolves around the family room, which often flows easily into the kitchen and dining areas. The fathers of Modernism—those schooled in the Bauhaus, such as Mies van der Rohe and Le Corbusier—envisioned optimal living environments as wide-open interior spaces. Flexible, practical, and filled with natural light, such spaces were considered highly utilitarian and often included built-in storage. Built-ins can be a blessing for a family room, since they'll hide clutter as you streamline this oft-used space. Even an antique cabinet can hold your children's toys.

The greatest design challenge here is the ubiquitous TV/entertainment center, which seems to get larger and larger over time. Camouflage that TV screen in a French armoire, or in one with a distressed or antiqued finish. Just remember to balance this large piece of furniture elsewhere in the room with an appropriately sized wall hanging, a grouping of small paintings, or a large bay window. Or, try incorporating the TV/entertainment center in built-in bookshelves.

LARGE OBJECTS—SUCH AS A GRAND PIANO—NEED TO BE BALANCED. IN THIS ROOM, THE PIANO IS BALANCED WITH THE BAY WINDOWS AND THE LARGE PAINTING.

FOR A FINISHED LOOK, USE LARGE
CABINETS AND WARDROBES TO HOUSE
TVS AND ENTERTAINMENT CENTERS.

formal living rooms

Some say we have forsaken our formal living rooms for the family room, yet the "parlor" of old offers the greatest opportunity to show off our prized collections. If we are fortunate enough to live in a home with substantial square footage, the formal living room can double as a gallery. This room is where the creative designer can "turn it on."

Your formal living space probably has some distinguishing architectural element. Start your design there. What is the first thing that you would like your guests to see? Your collection of African masks? Your Charles Eames furniture? If you are truly living in luxury, you will be able to establish more than one focal point.

FILL YOUR LIVING SPACE WITH CONTEMPORARY FURNITURE AND OBJECTS, YET KEEP THE TRADITIONAL FIREPLACE AS THE MAIN ATTRACTION. NOTICE THE MODERN TREATMENT OF VINTAGE ARCHWAYS.

AVOID CLUTTER, EVEN IN GENEROUS
LOFT SPACES. HERE, AN AIRY, MODERN
DAYBED COUNTERACTS A DENSE SOFA,
WHILE A PLAIN, DARK CABINET WITH
DELICATE JADE POTTERY BALANCES A
BOLD, CONCRETE FIREPLACE.

Use the simple forms, colors, and textures of Modern Nostalgia to spotlight the important design features. For instance, go completely contemporary except for the existing Victorian fireplace, which you can dress up with vintage candlesticks. Or, mix the chaise lounge with the white grand piano. Establish a mood by choosing your favorite traditional or exotic piece and surrounding it with two or three contemporary elements. Keep the composition simple.

BUILD THE ROOM LAYOUT AROUND THE MOST IMPORTANT OBJECTS—HERE, THE FIREPLACE SHARES CENTER STAGE WITH MODERN SCULPTURE. NOTICE THE INTERESTING COUNTERPOINT BETWEEN THE INTRICATE CHANDELIER AND SLEEK, CONTEMPORARY TABLE.

QUIRKY CLASSICS PUNCTUATE A CONTEM-
PORARY SETTING—AN OPEN, AIRY ATMOS-
PHERE AND THE GRAPHIC POWER OF
STRIPES HIGHLIGHT DECO TREASURES,
BUT KEEP THE MOOD MODERN.

dining rooms

Modern Nostalgia frees us from the rigid, traditional treatment of dining rooms. No longer must your dining chairs match your heirloom dining table. If they don't, and you feel uncomfortable about that, slip covers over them. You can even mix and match chairs from different periods. For instance, don't hesitate to flank a contemporary table with Chippendale chairs. Bear in mind that scale and proportion remain important, as do form and texture; upholstered seats don't mix well with wooden chair backs. Experiment, but stick to the basic guidelines suggested in Section One.

Dining rooms, like formal living rooms, have become somewhat neglected spaces—especially during the day. They often provide corners and wall areas for cabinets, hutches, paintings, or wall hangings. You also can use the table as a showcase for a special collection of glassware or fresh flowers. In the evening, the dimmed light of a modern or antique chandelier can enhance the mood of the room.

PLACE BOLD OBJECTS IN BOLD SPACES. THE DIMENSIONS OF THIS DINING ROOM ALLOWED FOR A LARGE TABLE AND SUBSTANTIAL LEATHER CHAIRS.

Display beauty in small doses. See how the lovely, natural wood of the circular Biedermeier table takes prominence in this dining room.

Formal dinner parties may have become a tradition of the past so that in fact frees up a room in your house to display your prized possessions. Design a built-in cabinet-shelving system for an entire wall of your dining room for your collection of vases and antique dishes, and photos of relatives. The room will seem clutter free while at the same time providing lots of show room. And the dining room walls can be a special gallery for your art collection. Recessed or track lighting can add a contemporary touch and also be a way to soften lighting during dining hours. The artwork, too, can be a source of conversation at the dinner table. Or, perhaps, turn the unused dining area into the work area you so desperately need.

THE CONTEMPORARY CHAIRS IN THIS DIN-
ING ROOM RELAX THE IMPOSING ARCHI-
TECTURE AND PRACTICALLY GUARANTEE
LIVELY DINNER PARTIES.

Use the formal dining room to showcase prized possessions, such as an antique Oriental cabinet and vases, and a gleaming silver tea set.

kitchens

Machine-age aesthetics changed kitchen design forever. Efficiency and cleanliness became prized as the use of industrial materials—stainless steel, concrete, wood, and marble—multiplied. In the modern kitchen, gadgetry can be celebrated or tucked away, while every tap, faucet, or cabinet is chosen with great care. Gaining sufficient natural or artificial lighting—especially over work surfaces—has become critical to kitchen design.

The present-day kitchen can be a gourmet cook's paradise. At the same time it is a relaxed space that combines elements of pleasure and recreation with those high-tech appliances. Nowadays, it's often a popular gathering place for family and friends, and even connected directly to the family room. It's not unusual then to add an easy chair in one corner, fill an antique American cupboard with decorative plates, or hang some pots and pans to give the room a personal touch.

TAKE THE DOORS OFF THE CUPBOARDS TO DISPLAY YOUR PLATES, SAUCERS, AND CUPS. THESE PIECES SEEM TO BE AS MUCH COLORFUL COLLECTIBLES AS THEY ARE DAILY DISHWARE.

LET THE PLETHORA OF MATERIALS IN THE CONTEMPORARY KITCHEN—WOOD CABINETS, MARBLE COUNTERS, STAINLESS STEEL APPLIANCES, AND WOOD FLOORS— MELD WITH ONE ANOTHER.

To lend a contemporary kitchen
the unexpected patina of age and
long use, give your kitchen cabinets
a distressed finish.

open homes: the modernist house

Study your entire house from different vantage points, and you may make surprising discoveries. Move from room to room and think about creating a visual flow throughout your home. Again, the goal is a light, airy interior that makes optimum use of available space, and provides a sleek, clutter-free environment. Does your living space now feel fresh and contemporary? Can you move easily from one room to the next? Do you feel connected to it through personal touches—antique furniture, special collections, art? Are you happy with the placement of the objects in the rooms? Do you experience visual drama and tension, but also find spaces for rest and contemplation? Are you happy with the lighting in the rooms?

If you've come this far and you are still dissatisfied, don't despair. Try this: Edit the room's furnishings to three essential pieces—two of them modern and one traditional. The old piece will bring character to the room, while the contemporary ones will streamline its appearance. Build from there, selectively adding just the necessary ingredients to complete the composition. Study the finished room under different lighting to gauge its overall effect. Then compare room to room. Eventually the whole will come together.

USE COLOR TO UNIFY A ROOM. HERE,
THE NATURAL COLOR OF THE WOODEN
BIEDERMEIER SOFA AND TABLE IS REPEAT-
ED IN THE PICTURE FRAMES AND ALSO IN
THE RUG AND LEOPARD PRINT PILLOW.

work spaces

The contemporary space for work at home is most often by the computer terminal. (Yet, even this is changing as technology goes wireless.) We've grown used to having a room, a corner, or at least a table for the computer. Handsome contemporary tables designed specifically for computers are available at furniture and office supply stores. Or choose an antique table for your computer terminal and place the table in your bedroom, family room, or den. Your work area can either dominate the space or simply be a small part of it. Sitting at a computer for long periods makes ergonomics especially important. For comfort, a keyboard needs to be at a certain height in relationship to your body. Having a highly flexible, ergonomic chair will allow you to place your computer on almost any type or height of surface. Your desk/table, no matter what vintage, should be relatively clutter free.

storage

If you've chosen the Modern Nostalgia look for your workspace, your computer may be on a sleek contemporary table, or perhaps an antique side table. The bulky desk is gone—and so that unnecessary storage space around it. Since the computer maintains most of your files, you won't need much paper anymore. Simply swivel your retro chair to find the stylish file cabinet set on casters for your convenience. Or turn behind you and open doors or drawers to the built-ins that sleekly line your den's walls. In other words, your workspace needn't be filled with papers and supplies. It can be free of needless clutter, so that your mind can be as creative and expansive as possible. On those shelves, place reminders of things past—mementos that can inspire you in your work, or simply bring you pleasure. And, perhaps, your office space can provide a delightful view of the world outside.

EASILY MAINTAIN AN UNCLUTTERED WORK SPACE WITH CONTEMPORARY BUILT-INS PERSONALIZED WITH TRADITIONAL ACCESSORIES.

Don't hesitate to place your computer on an antique French desk. Balance it with a lamp and a painting.

PARING DOWN

Perhaps Modern Nostalgia appeals to you, and you've just arranged a contemporary living space with a touch of the traditional. Yet, you can't quite get rid of the clutter— the little odds and ends, mementos, and the things of everyday life, such as magazines and books. How, you wonder, can your room look as clean and orderly as those in this book? Do people actually live in such neat, pristine spaces? Where is all their stuff?

The desire for a sleeker environment may stem from the image of a clutter-free space. And paring down the room isn't as hard one might think. Sometimes, we just have to sort through the objects around us and carefully place each one. Even the smallest object should receive your full attention. If we want to keep our collection of Grand-mother's pitchers in the living room, why not neatly line them up on a bookshelf? After all, those shelves can house our knickknacks as well as our books. Or why not cluster the collection of blue glass bottles on the fireplace mantle? Even unusual places, such as window alcoves and piano tops, can accommodate attractive vignettes. In short, clustering objects together saves room and can make the grouping art in itself.

Bearing in mind the principles of proportion and placement, you can imagine how even the smallest elements can fit into your living spaces. But don't saturate the room with them. Create interesting groupings and voids to balance the space. If you have too much stuff, change your arrangements seasonally.

It's also important to think about the activities that occur within each room. If you tend to consistently make clutter, create a place to store it so that your room can appear clutter free at the end of the day. For example, if someone often reads maga-zines in your living room, provide a nicely designed magazine rack for the magazines to gather in over time. Even kids' rooms can look neat when provided with a toy chest.

sleeping spaces

The rooms in which we sleep are now considered much more than just that. The bedroom has become a personal sanctuary, where we seek comfort and rest after a long day's work. Contemporary houses often provide huge master bedrooms with walk-in closets and spa-like bathrooms. At the same time, those of us who live in smaller urban dwellings may find our nighttime comfort in a cozier, yet just as welcoming, room that barely contains a queen-sized bed. The Modern Nostalgia rules are the same for the bedroom as they are for other spaces in our homes. Begin your plan with the most essential element, which in this case is usually the bed, and continue from there. Go for a mixture of the contemporary and the traditional, with the ultimate goal of a sleek, airy environment in mind. In the bedroom, the colors and textures of linens, curtains, and rugs play a significant role in setting the mood.

THE BEDROOM HAS BECOME OUR PERSONAL SANCTUARY. CONTEMPORIZE YOUR COMFORT ZONE, BUT RETAIN THE TOUCH OF TRADITION.

Tuck a bed under an eave for a feeling
of protection and coziness. Throw on
extra pillows for more comfort.

traditional beds

Despite your desire to go contemporary, the romantic in you yearns for the traditional, four-poster bed, a carved wooden sleigh bed, or a shiny brass headboard. Don't panic, though. The rest of the bedroom can be as modern as the bed is traditional. Begin with the bed covers. Choose sheets and quilts that display subtle contrasts in luxurious textures, but forgo the lace and ruffles of olden times. Patterns can be abstract or geometrically inspired and colors can be boldly displayed in large, chromatic blocks.

Or if you have a simple, nondescript bed and love that romantic draped look, throw mosquito netting or light, flowing fabric over the bed and create your own canopy. Be bold with your curtain materials.

If you have a traditional bed, the rest of the bedroom can be furnished and decorated in modern minimalism—a few simple chairs, lamps, and tables, along with your favorite wall hangings.

GIVE CONTEMPORARY BEDS A TRADITIONAL LOOK. YOU'LL NOTICE THAT THE BED ITSELF IS A PLATFORM BED, BUT THE ADDITION OF CURTAINS AT ITS HEAD AND THE PORTRAIT BRING AN ANTIQUE FEELING TO THE ROOM. ALSO, THE ARCHITECTURAL FEATURES AND THE STRAIGHT-BACK CHAIR GIVE THE ROOM TIMEWORN CHARM.

CREATE SUBTLE VISUAL DRAMA. THE
LINES OF THIS IRON-FRAMED BED ECHO
THOSE FOUND IN THE FIREPLACE FOR AN
INTERESTING SOLID/VOID STATEMENT

THE FOUR-POSTER BED STILL IS A COVET-
ED POSSESSION. HERE, WHITE CURTAINS
HUNG FROM SIMPLE WOODEN POSTERS
GIVE THE BED A FRESH LOOK.

modern beds

In modern times, the bed has grown wider, longer, and lower to the ground. Decorative frames have yielded to platforms or simple headboards that are sometimes made of wood or covered in fabric. To complement the spare bed, the purist may opt for built-in furniture throughout the room, assuring an uncluttered, lean décor.

Our contemporary vision has somewhat softened strict geometric lines. For instance, we might try to break the monotony of a long bed by placing an ottoman or chest at its foot or by covering the end of the bed with a colorful quilt or blanket. Differences in scale also help to break up a monotonous line. In fact, the scale of your reading tables in relationship to the bed is more important than is a contemporary match. So go ahead and use your Shaker table, as long as its height doesn't dwarf the bed. The style of lamp you set on that table will also help to define the mood of the bedroom.

CONTEMPORARY BEDS OFTEN INCORPORATE UPHOLSTERED HEADBOARDS AND FOOTBOARDS. THEY ALSO MAY BE FOOTED BY OTTOMANS OR TABLES. THESE ADDITIONS TO THE TYPICAL PLATFORM BED GIVE IT MORE HEIGHT.

Borrow from the Japanese tradition of minimalism. The bed, side tables, and lamps are simple in design and set low to the ground. The rest of the room is uncluttered.

other bedroom furniture

Larger bedrooms can serve as a laboratory for modern mixes, especially if your bed is contemporary. Try mixing and matching dressers and chests of different eras, or arrange a few chairs and tables to create a personal reading area. Use the scale, proportion, and color techniques that you've learned to establish the retreat that feels right for you. This is your most personal space. Remember to design it to be as clutter-free as possible, and each day you'll rediscover a small haven where you can quietly clear your mind.

There is no correct formula when matching bedroom chairs—whether you are matching contemporary with contemporary, contemporary with antique, or sophisticated with eccentric. Keep harmony in mind, but also remember that contrast sometimes can be pleasant. Now, examine the chair's shape. Is its back rounded or flat? Is its scale large and bulky, or fragile? If it is upholstered, do the covers match? Does the chair have arms? Try several arrangements.

DARE TO PAIR A MODERN BED WITH AN ANTIQUE CHAIR AND TABLE. HERE, A NEUTRAL PALETTE AND WEIGHTY TAUPE FABRICS CREATE A SOOTHING BACKGROUND FOR THE COLOR-RICH FURNISHINGS.

RULES OF PROPORTION APPLY TO THE
BEDROOM AS WELL. THE HEIGHT OF THIS
ANTIQUE CABINET IS OFFSET BY THE
HANGING PHOTOS ABOVE THE MODERN
BED FRAME. LAYERS OF PLUMP PILLOWS
BUILD UP THE HEAD OF THE BED AND
BALANCE IT AGAINST THE FOOT.

atmosphere

The bedroom is your most private sanctuary, and here, more than anywhere, you need to be aware that your design is establishing a mood. Modern Nostalgia can have a calming effect in the bedroom as it takes the clutter and extraneous details away from your personal haven. Clear the bedroom and clear the mind. Clutter-free, however, doesn't mean stark. The Modernists were particularly fond of Japanese compositions and sought exotic textures, materials, and colors in their designs. The idea is to create a welcoming atmosphere that is subtly sensual. Be indulgent with textures and colors.

As we regularly change our bed linens, so, too, can we can the mood in our bedchambers. Seasonally changes are obvious—wools in the winter and cottons in summer create coziness and breeziness. At the same time, extra down pillows or blankets in the winter or an antique quilt adds a special mood to the room in the winter. And, in the summer, it might be time to take out the silk sheets and candles.

EXPLICITLY ANNOUNCE THE MOOD OF YOUR BEDCHAMBER THROUGH YOUR CHOICE OF FURNITURE, AS SEEN HERE IN THE LEOPARD-SKINNED CHAIR AND EGYPTIAN-INSPIRED BED FRAME.

Atmosphere also can be established in more subtle ways—through careful attention to texture, color, light, and the harmonious placement of objects.

textures and materials

Modern Nostalgia glorifies surface textures—highly polished and beautifully jointed wooden floors, granite kitchen counters, marble tiles, stainless steel sinks and appliances, decorative plate glass, and brass stair railings. The materials, in themselves, become objects of our attention, especially when highlighted in our clutter-free environment. We praise the artisan of these materials.

Modern Nostalgia also encourages the juxtaposition of different surface materials—rough against smooth, concrete against velvet, silk against brick, and even voids against solids. These textures speak where intricate details of craftsmen once did. Try creating visual excitement by the juxtaposition of the subtler differences in textures used in rugs, curtains, and upholstery. Let your contemporary interiors reflect this in surprising ways.

CHOOSE A PRISTINE, NEUTRAL BEDCOVER
TO SET OFF THE COLORS AND TEXTURES
OF YOUR COLLECTIBLES AND FURNISHINGS.

RATHER THAN RELYING ON DRAMATIC
COLOR CHANGES FOR VISUAL EXCITE-
MENT, JUXTAPOSE DIFFERENT MATERIALS
AND TEXTURES.

bringing in color

Our goal in this modern age is to simplify, and colors can help us to do this. White is the quintessential backdrop for architecture and design, and it offsets individual blocks of bold colors to great advantage.

Contemporary design does not ignore the color wheel; in fact, the spirit of Modern Nostalgia offers both the neutral grays, whites, mauves, and tans, and the intense, bright colors in a range of fabrics and paints. Solid blocks of color are once again popular, and may be relieved by flashes of multicolored highlights, such as pillows, glass, fabric, wall hangings, curtains, and rugs. Today, color is used discretely as a tool for balancing a room or pulling objects together. Use color to establish the mood in a room—to enliven it or cool it down. Contemporary lighting effectively highlights your chosen colors.

DON'T BE AFRAID TO MIX BOLD COLORS IN YOUR BEDROOM. SUCH CONTRASTS GENERATE ENERGY AND EXCITEMENT.

NOTICE THE SUBTLE USE OF COLOR—
THE GRAY WALLS AND BEDCOVERING SET
AGAINST WHITE FURNISHINGS AND TRIM.

bathing spaces

Frankly, our contemporary definition of the ideal bathing space runs the gamut from the home luxury spa to the compact shower room. Of course, the choice may depend on the time of day (a quick shower in the morning before work or a relaxing whirlpool at night) or on the size of your home. Bathrooms increasingly are being custom designed so that each fixture or accessory is a design element in its own right. The traditional bathroom is making a comeback, but old-fashioned plumbing is not. And as our current definition is more eclectic, so is the *Modern Nostalgia* design concept. Almost anything goes in the bathroom, providing that the overall image is consistent. Keep marble with marble and wood paneling in its place. Mixing the contemporary and traditional is a challenge made easier by the general acceptance of an old friend—the claw-foot tub.

INDULGE IN AN ANTIQUE, FOOTED TUB
PLACED IN FRONT OF A LARGE WINDOW.

TRY A MORE RELAXED BATHROOM
ARRANGEMENT, AS SEEN HERE IN THE
ECLECTIC VANITY, SINK, STORAGE, MIR-
ROR, SCREEN, AND BASKETS NESTLED
BENEATH WOODEN BEAMS.

modern built-ins

Among its other innovations, the modern era introduced bathroom vanities. Built-ins streamlined the bath, bringing greater cleanliness and sanitary conditions to both the sink and tub areas. No one questioned that it was great to hide all that stuff away. Today, however, our love affair with vanities is lukewarm, particularly prefabricated ones. We often prefer built-ins made of luxurious woods or highly polished marbles that give our bathrooms a beautifully unique appearance. These surfaces can be especially becoming under artificial lighting that skillfully reflects the beauty of the wood or marble surface—and the human image in the mirror. Custom-designed built-ins can diminish the sense of architectural boundaries and can pull together otherwise bulky, unconnected fixtures. Along with built-ins came the use of large-surface mirrors. These mirrors are especially useful in expanding the dimensions of small bathrooms and bouncing light around the interiors.

THIS WOOD-ENCLOSED ROOM HAS A SEN-
SUOUS APPEAL, AND THE WOOD SERVES
TO HIDE THE BULKY CONTOURS OF THE
TUB AND SINK.

ENCASING YOUR TUB IN A WOODEN SUR-
ROUND GIVES IT RUSTIC APPEAL. SHINY
CHROME FIXTURES UPDATE THE LOOK.

the modern spa

Many opt for the soothing modern spa, which may include a whirlpool tub as well as a separate glass-enclosed shower. Go ahead—light the candles and turn on the jets. While most tubs and sinks are contemporary in style, many traditional pedestal sinks nonetheless find their way into modern spas. Cover the bathroom surfaces with contemporary tiles, yet hang an antique photo or picture to add a sense of tradition to the room.

Your bathroom can be dressed in contemporary or traditional details. Window blinds, for instance, make a much different statement than curtains do, and your dressing area can extend the contemporary look or be softened by an antique mirror.

A PORCELAIN PEDESTAL SINK LENDS A SLEEK, YET TIME-HONORED, IMAGE TO THE BATHROOM.

ALTHOUGH THIS BATHROOM RECALLS THE LOOK OF CLASSICAL ANTIQUITY, ITS CONTEMPORARY VANITY LOOKS RIGHT AT HOME.

CONSIDER LUXURY AS THE MAIN INGRED-
IENT FOR THE MODERN-DAY SPA. TRULY
SYBARITIC, THIS DRAMATIC, HIGH-
CEILINGED SPA SANCTIONS COMPLETE
SELF-INDULGENCE.

old-fashioned tubs

The diversification in our bathing spaces brings a shower to one bathroom and an antique, claw-footed tub to another. Of course, a footed bathtub makes a strong design statement, so you may want to finish the rest of the room traditionally. But why not be a bit eclectic? Surround the tub with contemporary materials—marble tiles and a sleek sink. Create a corner gallery of your favorite beaded handbags or a collection of exotic seashells.

CHOOSE YOUR CLAW-FOOTED TUB FROM MYRIAD CONTEMPORARY COLORS. IN THIS CASE, THE DEEP RED OF THE TUB IS CAPTURED IN THE RICH DRAPERY FABRIC.

THE OLD-FASHIONED TUB HAS MADE
A COMEBACK, AND IT DOESN'T EVEN
NEED ITS TRADITIONAL FEET. DON'T
BE FOOLED, HOWEVER. THE PLUMBING
IS AS UP-TO-DATE AS CAN BE.

LIGHTING

We can't establish the ideal Modern Nostalgia environment without discussing lighting. For how can we enjoy the pleasures of all our work, if we can't see it clearly? Proper lighting of our environment is crucial, and it's important to consider day and evening lighting. That means both natural and artificial. In our design scheme we need to consider lighting levels and colors, lighting sources, and the use of old-fashioned versus contemporary lamps.

Your choice will depend, of course, upon the activities in the room. In a kitchen, track lighting is desirable above a countertop. Contemporary track lighting or recessed is a delightful design solution that is most invisible. In the dining room, you may choose an antique fixture for its traditional value. Remember dimming controls can establish varying moods. Spotlights can be used to highlight prized antique possessions. Lamps can also be chosen purely for decoration.

MODERN**FUSION**

With globe-trotting on the rise and the World Wide Web in our homes, most of us have delighted in a multitude of cultures. And in our travels we have become, through repeated exposure, design hunters and gatherers, bringing treasures, new color palettes, and ideas back to our nests.

There was a time when these treasures sat tucked away because they did not match our home's architectural style or its furnishings. A Country home, for instance, would never display a Parisian, red velvet loveseat next to an old Shaker rocker.

Thankfully, those limitations are a thing of the past! Now, we are embracing a new design process that fuses the myriad elements of world style. We're opting more for the surprising and the unconventional, and less for familiar, but boring, proper matches.

This chapter will help you to marry diverse styles and unconventional elements. Ultimately, you will achieve a new take on your favorite style, whether it be country, romantic, classic, or eclectic. Its fusion with modernity will give your home the best of both worlds.

country · romantic · classic · eclectic

BRING TOGETHER TRADITIONAL STYLE
AND A MODERN LAYOUT FOR ROOMS
THAT ARE EASY ON THE EYE—AND EASY
TO LIVE IN.

modern country

When we say modern style, it conjures up descriptors like sleek, clean, smooth, simple, and angular. But if you look at some country styles with an eye toward mixing them with modern, the same adjectives apply. Shaker furniture is the perfect example of that, with its straight lines. For the most part, merging Country with Modern in your rooms gives you the chance to juxtapose old with new while maintaining the warmth that comes with the Country style.

working with accessories

Think about how interesting your rooms will look merging the sleek lines of contemporary pieces with the curves and carvings that were emphasized on chair backs, and table legs from the nineteenth century. A few antique accessories can bring in just enough nostalgia to warm a modern room without making it seem period in style. Try bringing in small groups of quirky objects, such as antique sugaring tins. Display them in groupings of three or five on window sills or the tops of contemporary cabinets. Fill them with colorful dried flowers or grass to add depth and dimension.

Old stained glass windows are another good starting point for a single-room accessory to highlight in a modern mix. Pair that with a clean-lined windowsill that you've painted with a high-gloss primary color. To add more interest, introduce a contemporary chair nearby that's also covered in an energetic fabric pattern. When easing into Modern style, it is especially important to edit out fabrics with small or floral patterns: Solid colors, large blocks of color, and patterns with large, bold repeats automatically present a contemporary look, even when paired with vintage Country furnishings.

REMEMBER, HOME DESIGN WITHOUT SURPRISES, HUMOR, AND WHIMSY MAKES A DULL, RIGID SPACE! THINK ABOUT HOW MUCH YOU MIGHT ENJOY INTEGRATING A LITTLE OF THE UNEXPECTED—SUCH AS THIS MARBLE BUST. THE REST OF THE ROOM IS A MODERN COUNTRY CLASSIC WITH ALL THE MUST-HAVES: WHITE FLOOR BOARDS AND WALLS, PALE WOOD, THE NATURAL TEXTURES OF COIR AND WICKER, AND A SIMPLE, PARED DOWN DESIGN.

HOW CAN YOU FEED YOUR PASSION FOR
CLEAN AND CONTEMPORARY WHILE FUL-
FILLING YOUR LOVE OF COUNTRY STYLE?
USE AN ALL-WHITE TREATMENT TO SEAM-
LESSLY BLEND THE TWO. NOTICE HERE
HOW THE WORN WOOD AND DETAILS
OF THE PITCHER COLLECTION SHOW UP
BEAUTIFULLY AGAINST THE NATURAL
WOOD SHELVING, YET THE PALE, MONO-
CHROMATIC PALETTE GIVES THESE
ROOMS AN OVERALL MODERN FEELING.

themes and collections

A simple theme or collection of interesting objects with a past can work well to fuse Country style and modern décor. Consider a single color and a single object theme—all white (which is always modern) with, for example, pails, pitchers, or dishes that can be tucked into a modern cubby or on simple shelving. As a harmonious focal point add textural interest by stacking a basket collection nearby.

For fun, the next time you go to a flea market, head for the kitchen gadget section. Gather up a bunch of old eggbeaters, wooden spoons, or even measuring cups, and think about how they could add just the right dimension and warmth to a cool stainless steel kitchen—especially if you display them in an unexpected way. For example, you could group them on a wall in a loose pyramid. The key to off-center displays is to keep the number of objects an odd number rather than an even one. Try to avoid symmetry (which makes collections look dull) in your display approach: stagger the objects directly on a wall, or install stepped shelves (longest length on the bottom, shortest at the top) and climb the collection from one shelf to the next.

To blend in Country antiques, many interior designers use them as stand-ins for paintings and art. Try the art gallery trick of painting walls a bright hue (yellow works especially well) as a backdrop for a large antique or collection of antique objects. Naïve groupings such as large farm implements can be arranged all the way up a stairwell in place of prints or framed artwork.

Nor is imperative that your collection be truly antique, quirky items such as glass bottles can bring an antique point of view to the corner of a room. Choose a place where light can shine through the colored glass, or display them in the bath along the countertop or near the tub. The shiny surfaces of tile and ceramic will highlight the bottle's different shapes, colors, and sizes.

weaving together old and new

If you just think about creating special little views for yourself, you can create a design plan that weaves your cherished old pieces in with the new. Think function and design together. For example, if you have a small room (perhaps a laundry) that you've painted all white, it would be the perfect place to warm up with five or six of your favorite cross-stitched antique linen towels. Frame them in old or contemporary frames to add color, texture, and a pleasant visual that merges the past with the present.

Continue this theme by taking old prints and putting them in new frames or taking new prints and putting them in old frames. Subject matter can vary from old family photos that could fill up a bedroom wall to pictures from a recent trip abroad, which would be the perfect fit on a library wall.

Do the same with mirrors. Get a rhythm going in a tiny powder room with a mix of Shaker-style framed mirrors and put them next to some old flea market finds framed in pine or oak. Stack them in threes or create an interesting shape on the wall.

SOMETIMES YOU NEED ONLY ONE OR TWO
DESIGN ELEMENTS TO ACHIEVE THE MOD-
ERN COUNTRY LOOK. IN THIS CASE, THE
WARM, PINE FLOOR SUPPORTS A SHAKER
STYLE BEDROOM SET GONE CONTEMPO-
RARY. THE SIMPLICITY OF THE SNOW-
WHITE BED, TOPPED WITH A SUBTLY
COLORED QUILT AND TENTED IN A SIMPLE
STRIPED COTTON, EXEMPLIFIES THE HAR-
MONIOUS BLENDING OF TWO STYLES.

city walls, country floors

A key component to creating a modern Country look is visual tension: when mixing old and new, keep in mind that the more contrast you have, the better. Consider creating some drama by making a large component of the room (the floor) feel very antique, while mixing it with a very updated wall color, furnishings, or fabric. Rather than leaving the floor bare wood, pattern it with stain or paint to mimic a favorite Country quilt or other fabric in the room. You might even want to pick up a Country pattern and simply use it as a border around the perimeter of the room.

To adapt a pattern from a quilt—a crisp hexagon or a bright red tulip, for example—center geometric elements (the hexagon), and let figured elements (the tulip) work off center. Choose dark colors if you want the pattern to sit back, and bright ones, if you want to really call out the theme.

For walls, consider bright white, which has two advantages: it always adds a contemporary dose of atmosphere, yet it emphasizes the warm tones in Country-style wooden pieces. Explore the possibility of painting a single wall a bright primary red or yellow as a backdrop to play up an interesting country treasure, or to create an intimate corner for conversation and reading. To weave in bright color a bit more, stencil a bold geometric pattern at ceiling height. Or, create an energized wall where Country and Modern merge via a mix of picture frames. Set sleek, high-gloss black frames next to intricately carved oaks.

Bring in an element of surprise by using Country-style hand-hooked rugs as wall hangings that share the view with a contemporary dining table. Or use an antique hooked rug as a wall hanging next to an old pine table that's been painted snow white.

YOU CAN EASILY MAINTAIN THE COUNTRY LOOK WITHOUT GIVING UP MODERN NECESSITIES AND CONVENIENCES. YOU CAN DO THIS BY KEEPING THE OLD PINE FLOORS AND CEILING TRUSSES IN THEIR NATURAL STATE WHILE BUILDING IN COMPLEMENTARY COMPONENTS. NOTICE HOW THE WHITE BEAD BOARD AND SLATE ON THE TUB AND SINK ENHANCE THE AUTHENTIC COUNTRY ATMOSPHERE.

USE THE MODERN APPEAL OF PURE WHITE
TO BRING DIFFERENT FURNITURE STYLES
TOGETHER. HERE, WHITE WORKS WELL
TO ENHANCE THE COUNTRY FEELING OF
THE SIDEBOARD, WHILE NEATLY HIGH-
LIGHTING THE CLASSIC SHAPES OF THE
TABLE AND CHAIRS. A GEOMETRICALLY
STAINED FLOOR PATTERN, PLAIN UPHOL-
STERY, AND AN UPDATED WALL COLOR
GIVE THE ROOM MODERN APPEAL WITH-
OUT SACRIFICING A WARM, COUNTRY
ATMOSPHERE.

sleek meets antique

Sleek, contemporary architecture punctuated with pure Country-style doors or frames can make a wonderful, eye-pleasing combination. Don't be afraid to work with fairly large pieces such as antique, Country-style doors—which can be hung on contemporary closet frames, or used as panels for a screen. If carpentry is not a challenge, choose a different antique replacement for each closet door: there is more impact added through repetition.

Architectural detail is a great way to merge periods in an interior design. Especially in Country-style mixes, it is quite easy to locate large pieces such as supports, window frames, and doors, that can be recycled as a decorative element. Look for dealers who specialize in reclaimed items—the options are amazing: barn floors; staircases, lighting fixtures, mantels, soapstone sinks, antique stoves, and even floor tiles from old homes. Old soapstone sinks are wonderful in a modern kitchen design, as are recycled tiles. Try them as a backsplash, or use them on countertops, in front of the kitchen sink, or to box in a bathtub.

country style, without clutter

As you move through this chapter you will see how simple, uncluttered rooms enhance compatibility of modern Country combinations. You will also see that painting Country-styled furniture white brings on a crisp, updated modern feeling—all the while emphasizing the craftsmanship and unique lines of the furnishings. Make note too how all-white walls give these details center stage.

It will quickly become apparent that you can get modern design elements to sit back in your room schemes by using neutrals and/or white as the main palette, and, you can bring modern forward, and have Country elements be more functional, dovetailing with the period of the room.

There's also a practical element in this style of decorating. If you scour flea markets and find pieces you truly love but they are badly stained, or the styling is too heavy for your home, painting the pieces in bright or neutral colors will hide flaws and update the look. Whatever way you choose to decorate, modern Country lets you build the texture of your rooms via your travels to antique stores, flea markets, and showrooms.

Let contemporary furnishings and accents enter the neutral zone. Here, black accents show in stark relief against plain wood and white walls, and the modern, off-white lamp and chair don't detract from this countrified sitting room.

modern romantic

The beauty of dovetailing romantic with modern styles in your home is that you can introduce a dynamic interplay of shapes and colors, and ultimately create a room with engaging, richly textured vistas. Remember that by placing detailed period pieces next to clean, straight-lined modern furnishings or art, you can emphasize the best attributes of each. The same holds true with fabrics, lighting and accessories.

Perhaps this idea of modern romantic appeals to you, but you need a little design jump start on just how to create successful combinations.

Following are some ways to think about what you might do, and in what order. The easiest approach to this type of change is to look at the largest design elements of a room (walls, floors, windows) first, then consider furnishings, fabrics, lighting and accessories.

modern walls, romantic atmosphere

You can capture a contemporary feeling on your walls and keep romance in the air by juxtaposing a modern palette with romantic furniture. Any ornate or baroque looking piece will look terrific against a powerful wall color like lilac or tomato red. These days, color experts and trend watchers tell us bright colors are in, including the lime greens, purples, and bright yellows of the 1960s. If this is appealing, consider making the walls of your home the backdrop for your modern romantic mix. Imagine for a minute the visual drama you would create setting your French Provincial, eighteenth-century style Louis XV commode basking in the glow from a Tuscan yellow wall. Make the scene even more contemporary and toss some oversized pillows on the floor that have been covered in red and white polka dots.

 The wonderful thing about blending Romantic style into a more modern setting is that the combination can serve to heighten the romantic atmosphere. Consider keeping one wall true to period detail by using wallpaper prints that reflect romance— florals or country scenes; or by covering the wall with a flourish of silk brocade. Keep surrounding walls contemporary, in color and finish, and the result is a dramatic window on the romance of bygone eras—nicely set off by the coolness of more contemporary surroundings. Embellish this area of the room by adding antique fabrics to pillows or chairs with contemporary lines.

WITHOUT THESE TWO CONTEMPORARY
VASES ON THE OLD MARBLE MANTEL, THE
VIEW WOULD NOT BE AS ENGAGING. AND
THE ANTIQUE MIRROR, PAINTED A CON-
TEMPORARY WHITE, LENDS THE COMPOSI-
TION A ROMANTIC AIR.

YOU CAN USE ANTIQUE PIECES TO GREAT
EFFECT IN A CONTEMPORARY BATH.
HERE, THE INTERESTING PATTERNS AND
SHAPES OF THE OLD METAL URN, TEAPOT,
AND PLASTER SCULPTURE WORK WELL
AGAINST THE STONE WALL CAPPED WITH
DENTIL MOLDING. ANY ATTRACTIVE COL-
LECTIBLE CAN BE A PART OF THE SCENE.

windows: the modern romance of light and fabric

Contemporary window treatments run the gamut from simple wood shutters to volumes of fabric (silk, linen, cotton) tossed over hooks to frame the windows like thick frosting. How you create your look depends on whether you want to maintain the view at all times or want the option of darkening the room. Beyond that, window treatments are wonderfully flexible in the number of style solutions they offer: if your beloved antique heirloom is fine draperies rather than fine furniture, they can look wonderful paired with the edgy shapes of modern classic furniture.

Bring in lengths of lined fabrics that can be twisted and turned around a window's frame, or big, formal, ball-gown tiebacks, with acres of extra yardage. Set the stage with florals, brocades, or gauzy lace, and then keep the players (the furnishings) plain, pure, and simple. The romantic excesses at the windows will infuse the room with nostalgic presence, but allow its floor plan to stay practical, uncluttered, and modern. Keep in mind that the heavier the fabric, and the more fabric used, the more the romantic mood surfaces.

Since Romantic style can also be thought of as light, gauzy, and pale, it is easy to find good chemistry between lacy and translucent window treatments, and clean-lined, contemporary layouts. Again, generous yardage of the fabric of choice remains key, as does a slightly less tidy approach: think of floor skimming, pooling, and billowing lengths of the lightest lace and gauze. Then strive to keep the rest of the elements in the room modern and trim.

Last, if you've opted to use the walls (including windows) as modern contrast for baroque furnishings, it is easy to choose materials and shapes that will emphasize contemporary over anything else. Today rings, and ties, and pooling fabric below the window are popular, and these simple, tidy looks work perfect in contrast to the high-detail romantic furnishings you will place nearby.

SOMETIMES WINDOWS BECOME THE CEN-
TER OF ATTENTION AS THEY DO HERE,
WITH YARDS OF FABRIC EMPHASIZING THE
ROMANTIC MOOD.

plain floors, pure romance

Whether your space is brimming with romantic antiques or heirlooms, you can instantly
modernize the whole space without having to let go of a single one. Freshen the look
by stripping away rugs and keeping the floor bare, or by changing the floor surface
from hardwood to tile, stone, or ceramic. The smooth hard surface will provide an
immediate and unique visual frame for the abundance of shapes, fabrics and wood
surfaces in furniture collection. Likewise the contrast of warm woods and luxurious
fabrics on the cool stone can make what was once a cozy room seem grand.

stones with a past

For those who prefer a less dramatic look, moving from hardwood to antique stone,
like terra cotta or limestone, streamlines and modernizes a nostalgic room-without
straying too far from romance. Look, for example, at the many new options that
mimic the worn, smooth beauty of old stone floors found in chateaus, abbeys, and
churches. You can even find versions of real limestone studded with 3-million year old
fossils. Carved wood pieces from any period sit wonderfully against plain or polished
stone, and even the most antique-cluttered room feels instantly updated.

finishing touches

Once a room has a good framework for modern romance-plain walls paired with
ornate treasures; ornate windows teamed with sleek furnishings; or polished bare
floors showing off antique and heirloom finds- accents may be carefully added to
emphasize areas and add texture. Furniture fabrics, lighting, and accessories can
achieve the same modern design balance, and maintain the romantic focus you love.
Again, much depends on where romantic design elements are found in the room.
Contemporary fabrics and patterns, can, for example, bring new life to an antique
loveseat or day bed that is framed in a heavy, detailed carved base. The key here is to
heighten the element of surprise (if you opt for colors, keep them strong and saturated; if texture is the essential, make it sinfully rich) and let go of old design "rules" that
have kept you on the "matching path" too long! Have some fun. Hold on to that old
settee-but jolt it into the present.

REMEMBER THAT CONTEMPORARY FUR-
NISHINGS, SUCH AS THIS WIRY, MIDNIGHT
BLACK DINING SET CAN WORK WELL ON
THEIR OWN—ALLOWING COLORFUL,
ROMANTIC DETAILS TO CATCH YOUR
ATTENTION. CONSIDER SEGREGATING
THE MODERN FROM THE ROMANTIC
WHEREVER YOU WANT TO EMPHASIZE
EACH STYLE'S UNIQUE FORM.

MONOCHROMATIC COLOR THEMES HELP
TO BLEND PERIOD STYLES. WHITE-ON-
WHITE KEEPS THE MOOD SERENE IN THIS
PARLOR, AND MARRYING PERIOD CHAIRS
WITH A WHITEWASHED COUNTRY TABLE
GIVES ROMANCE THE LEADING ROLE.

lighten the mood

Imagine changing the setting in a Victorian-style room by hanging a contemporary chandelier over the table. Perhaps the room has chairs with a shell or leaves carved in the backs; track down contemporary lighting with versions of shell and leaf shapes and add it to the room. Lighting is an especially good place to let imagination, playfulness, and an airy design play off heavier furnishings. Take the same approach with lighting for occasional tables in the hall or beside the bed. The contrast of thick and thin angles, heavy materials and light, as well as opaque and translucent materials will breath new life into your romantic styling.

sleekness is in the details

Well-chosen accessories can bring a room a long way toward a more updated style, without watering down the romance of a beloved interior. Weaving in contemporary glass art, or photography for example, is an interesting, effective way to get a modern romantic look. Sleek, sculptural modern glass brings a presence all its own to a room. Perhaps replacing a fussy, ornate table lamp with one of clear, hand blown glass is all a particular corner needs to feel pulled-together. Likewise, an assemblage of black-and-white photos in contemporary frames can make a bland wall the focus of attention. For the best display, keep the matting white, frames simple and black, and arrange pictures in odd-numbered groupings. Add even more drama by bringing in a single, large piece of contemporary art in an otherwise vintage mix; the contrast will refresh and stimulate.

In all Modern Romantic blends, don't worry about making a perfect balance between the number of pieces in each style: Look first at what you have of each, and always begin with a layout that suits the room. Never treat a room like a puzzle into which all the pieces *must* fit—that is the first misstep toward uncomfortable interiors that look "arranged" and feel stagnant. Experiment to find the best floor plan, even if that means leaving out one or two larger pieces of furniture. Then gather inspiration from the rich beauty each style has to offer, and mix and match to your heart's content.

When you're debating about what to mix with what and where to place them, remember to consider views to the rooms beyond. Here, a stunning antique chest of drawers displays a romantic, yet modern collage while enhancing the view to the next room. These little islands of contrast color your space and can serve several purposes.

Borrowing on classic lessons in balance and symmetry, you can indulge your dual passions for modern and romantic styles with a few rich pieces that make simple statements.

DISPLAYING COLLECTIONS

The thoughtful arrangement of collections and decorative objects can change a room dramatically and enhance its atmosphere and personality. Collections come in myriad shapes and sizes—whether baskets, coins, sculpture, glassware, or other treasures. The key to blending them in to a Modern atmosphere is the art of display. Here are a few pointers for achieving the perfect look.

single treasures —displaying a single prized piece

The best (and commonsense) way to highlight a single large piece is to make it a focal point. Locate the largest expanse of wall in the room, or use the fireplace mantle (since the fireplace is nearly always the focal point of the room) for display. In a living room that is broken up by many windows with no clear center of attention, let the piece be freestanding (if possible) next to the sofa or central seating area.

gathering and grouping

If you have a varied range of objects, group them with an eye toward one feature that links them all together. Whether color, size, or material, this approach will make for a more coherent display. For collections or treasures that are few in number, use the rule of odd numbers, grouping in threes, fives, sevens, and so on. Odd numbers have more visual impact than even numbers. Place repetitive objects (plates of the same size or figurines of identical height, for example) in an ordered row, for a formal and striking display. Mix heights for collections of two or three objects (this works especially well for simple shapes) and place the grouping off-center on a mantle, windowsill, or shelf for impact.

For framed objects, place them last in the room. The height and width of other furnishings, and even the draperies, will change to look of a hanging display. Traditional wisdom advises placing any hanging display at eye level, but this rule can be broken to good effect. Place pictures over a loveseat or sofa slightly lower than eye level to create an intimate and inviting area. Emphasize a chair rail—or mimic one—by hanging pictures just above the top edge. Highlight a door by hanging a small picture above it.

decorator secrets

Sometimes the most stylish displays are objects shown in a new way. Take cues from an old French tradition and hang a favorite platter with a wide ribbon. Simply loop a length of ribbon through a metal ring, and sew the ends together. Repeat with another length of ribbon, then slide the platter through the loops and hang the ring on a picture hook.

Display collections of beautiful antique linens, napkins, or handkerchiefs by framing them behind glass. Small squares and rectangles work best: simply wash and starch, then center on the frame board, as you would a picture, and make sure the edges of the board are not showing. Mount carefully into the frame (watch out for wrinkles) and arrange on the wall.

modern classic

The décor combo called Modern Classic emphasizes the best attributes of classic and modern design—with shapes and colors for the ultimate in drama and staying power.

Feel free to introduce an unconventional design detail that shakes up the view—mixing traditional furnishings with new pieces of different styles and origins (Modern, French, Scandinavian, Italian, Swedish), as opposed to decorating with cookie-cutter suites of furniture. Introduce unexpected dashes of bright color or art to enhance the look of a bedroom or bath. Modern Classic, like the classic "little black dress" coupled with red shoes, always works; always gets noticed; and always lets your individuality come through.

As you move through this chapter, take note of the important role positioning has to play. Good positioning makes classic rooms artistic and magnificent. As professional interior designers advise, allow the whole rather than its parts to stand out.

Just as in any décor combinations (from Modern Country to Modern Romantic,) the recipe for success with Modern Classic is in subtle mixes and bold strokes. There are unlimited possible combinations, but the watchword for Modern Classic is refined.

For someone who thinks outside the box, any room can be an artist's canvas. And an artist it was, perhaps, who designed this room, which features striking contemporary interpretations of classical elements. The red wall's strong color lends drama to the composition.

high classic/low modern — easing in

This combination gives your cherished classically designed rooms a hint of modern, bringing in fresh zones of color, light, and texture. It's the bridge that may eventually take you to an entirely new style. A good first step is to review the major design components of one room you would like to work on.

BREAK THE BALANCE: If you can, look at the room according to areas of use. For example: conversation area, reading corner, a sunny window garden, and so on. Next, review the components of each area. Perhaps the layout has a wooden coffee table, two couches facing each other, one brass floor lamp, and two wooden side tables with brass lamps. Everything is balanced and nothing is really unexpected in the scene.

MIXING IN MODERN: Add some modern elements will alter that scene and bring in a new, energized atmosphere. Consider replacing a large wooden piece (perhaps the coffee table) in order to lighten the look. Even simply adding a glass or limestone top to an existing table will do much to reinvent the room.

LET BALANCE AND SYMMETRY HELP YOU
TO MERGE THE CLASSIC AND CONTEMPO-
RARY. YOU CAN HAVE EAST MEETS
WEST... BRITAIN MEETS AFRICA, AND
SO ON; JUST KEEP THE LAYOUT SIMPLE
AND CLEAN, AND THE COMBINATIONS
WILL WORK.

reinvent the table

A Modern Classic piece that is timeless and elegant can easily be made with some reclaimed architecture. Try seeking out a classic, wooden fluted column (either an authentic building artifact or a reproduction) and using it as a dining table base. Limestone or marble are the perfect complement as a top, Though not for the faint of heart—or short of construction savvy—the resulting modern classic treasure is worth the effort.

A simpler approach for the same kind of design impact involves mixing chair styles in seating areas: place Modern style upholstered chairs among classic, straight-backed chairs (if they are antiqued with white and gold, so much the better). Keep the palette soft, or use rich purples and pinks to add whimsy.

turn architecture upside down

Creating tension with different heights is another technique for stepping into classic modern style—and for curing an overly symmetrical room. If side tables are present, make them a home for complementary modern lamps of two different heights. Seed the room with large elements given a new use: a Palladian window might become a tabletop; an old door, a desktop, and so on. Introducing very large pieces (columns, or a mirror) can have an added benefit for small rooms: the unexpectedly large scale of the elements is a trompe l'oeil that will make the room feel larger.

HERE, A CLASSIC FLUTED COLUMN DOES DOUBLE DUTY AS A PEDESTAL TABLE. PALE COLORS MAKE A PERFECT BACKDROP FOR THIS MIX OF CLASSIC FURNISHINGS AND PARED-DOWN, MODERN SENSIBILITY.

HERE IS AN EXAMPLE OF HOW, BY POSI-
TIONING BELOVED OLD CLASSICS IN AN
ALCOVE OR CORNER, A ROOM CAN
ACHIEVE MODERNITY AND STILL RETAIN
POCKETS OF TREASURE. BECAUSE THE
GLASS ORNAMENTS, BELL JAR, AND SHAPE-
LY LAMPS ARE TUCKED AWAY FROM THE
REST OF THE ROOM, THE DESIGN CAN
DISCREETLY MERGE CLASSIC AND MODERN
ELEMENTS. THE LOOK IS UPDATED WITH
CONTEMPORARY PIECES THROUGHOUT
THE REST OF THE ROOM.

subtle details

CHANGE THE MOOD OF A LIVING SPACE
THROUGH ITS LIGHTING. REGULATE NAT-
URAL LIGHT WITH BLINDS AND DRAPERIES
TO CREATE DIFFERENT ATMOSPHERES
DURING THE DAY. AT NIGHT, CHANGE
THE MOOD WITH THE SOFT, DIFFUSED
LIGHT OF A DECORATIVE CHANDELIER OR
THE WARM, ROMANTIC GLOW OF A FIRE-
PLACE AND CANDLES.

At its best, Classic style often relies on elegant symmetry. Good mixes of Modern
and Classic style add a bit of personality and energy to the Classic tradition through
quirky details. An elegant monochromatic color palette smoothed over a suite of
unmatched chairs, for example. Or a collection of antiquities displayed in an industrial modern interior. Surprisingly, much of the material used in modern design
makes a fine match for vintage treasures. If you collect sculpted pieces, it is interesting to pair an ancient carved Buddha, for example, with the very modern limestone
flooring of a loft.

KEEPING THE PALETTE SIMPLE MAY HELP
THE MOST AS YOU PLAN YOUR MODERN
CLASSIC ROOM. HERE, PLUM AND GOLD
MAINTAINS THE CONTEMPORARY FEEL OF
THIS SITTING ROOM, AND THE TRIO OF
MODERN ART IN THE SAME PALETTE
WORKS PERFECTLY WITH THE CLASSIC
SEATING. NOTICE, TOO, HOW THE OFF-
WHITE WALL AND CEILING SHOWCASE
THE CEILING TRIM.

classic colors

Consider bringing forward the classic architectural details to frame modern groupings of furniture. Paint with an eye toward outlining and bringing details forward in the room. Don't get bogged down in thinking that Modern looks can only be successful with bright colors; a light or pale palette often works better to blend these two styles. Intensity plays a big role in using color correctly; the tricks is to aim for nuanced palettes that pick up and repeat soft tints in furnishings and accessories. Since "soft" can easily become "weak," try deepening color as you move toward the floor: lightest tints on the ceiling, more color in the walls, a bit more in the window and furniture fabrics, and the deepest hue along the baseboards.

As you blend Modern and Classic pieces, don't be in a hurry for radical change. Follow your instincts, and proceed slowly. Most important, if an update feels contrived, awkward or overdesigned to you, then avoid it—however stylish it is rumored to be. The idea of easing some modern into a classically styled home is to find modern components you love, and will enjoy looking at in your nest. No one is keeping score; the balance is up to you.

DRAW ATTENTION TO THE TINIEST, MOST
OBSCURE PLACES IN YOUR ROOMS. THESE
CLASSIC AND MODERN COLLECTIONS
CLIMB UP A NARROW SHELF, ADDING
COLOR AND TEXTURE TO THE SPACE.
TAKE ADVANTAGE OF CUBBYHOLES AND
CORNERS; TURN THEM INTO DIMINUTIVE
HAVENS FOR DESIGN.

modern eclectic

If you were to undertake a recipe from a renowned French chef, the process might seem endless, but each ingredient would serve a very special purpose in the overall flavor. Likewise, the components in a room categorized as Modern Eclectic could very well come from a great design chef. But lucky for the latter, he or she can turn up the heat on color, texture, and variety and never really ruin the room.

Move a chair, remove a piece of pottery, tweak here and there, and all is well. This is, more than anything, design from the soul, a collection of treasures from the past and present on one visual plane. Mixing Modern and Eclectic styles brings variety that will energize rooms, and add dimension and inspiration to décor. Modern Eclectic style will transform a room into a place that is both simple and sophisticated, and in touch with fundamental pleasures.

THE CONTEMPORARY TONE OF THIS ROOM IS SOFTENED WITH THE NATURAL COLORS AND TEXTURES OF WOOD. AN ASSORTMENT OF ANIMAL FIGURINES GIVES THE SPACE CHARACTER, AS DOES THE DUBIOUS-LOOKING FISH PRESIDING OVER THE DINING TABLE.

Think of each corner of a room as a little canvas that tells a story. Perhaps it's a tale of your travels as told through art or furnishings. Be brave; mix styles, colors, and shapes to give your vignette life and personality.

easing into modern style

This is probably the easiest design scheme to accomplish because you can ease into modern at any intensity that is comfortable. So, again, what works best in a Modern Eclectic approach is to explore the world of modern but continue to celebrate the pleasure of things from the past. This is use what you have decorating at its best. The fundamental secret is the same as with the other styles—good editing—but blending modern style with an eclectic mix offers the most design freedom. Choose your favorite treasures and combine them with just enough modern style for comfort, practicality, and good looks.

Look at candidates for change and revision—walls, windows, fabrics, art, and furnishings. Walk around your rooms and see how you can improve the view from a variety of angles.

IF YOUR HEART IS DIVIDED AND YOU LOVE THE LOOK OF FADED AUBUSSON OR OLD WORLD RUGS AS MUCH AS YOU LOVE SPLASHY MODERN SHAPES AND FABRICS, THERE IS A WAY TO SUCCESSFULLY COMBINE THE TWO. MATCH THE RUG'S FADED COLOR PALETTE WITH THE SAME HUES ELSEWHERE, BUT TURN UP THEIR VOLUME; USE THESE COLORS AT FULL SATURATION IN THE ACCESSORIES, PILLOWS, AND UPHOLSTERY.

Here old and new live in harmony
and collectibles such as hand blown
glass balloons and an old bell merge
beautifully in an eclectic room.

eclectic basics

Because Eclectic style, by its very nature, is a real mix—it may be hard to sort out where to begin. Perfectly "set" styles (such as a room that is completely Mission) can look contrived: but without careful planning, eclectic rooms can lose focus and simply look cluttered. Here are a few design keys to help you work:

style mix

Try to keep the number of completely different styles in the room (French Country, Japanese, Victorian) to three to five. Balance the look by including at least two items that are from a similar style or period.

individual details

Details are the secret bridge that can bring a design together. If you can identify a simple common element, such as a curve, it can be capitalized on throughout the room. For example, highlight the shape of a room with a curving alcove by choosing a curve front dresser, oval rather than rectangular occasional tables, curved mirrors, and carved or sculpted pieces (whether furniture or accessories) that echo this shape.

HIGHLIGHT THE COMMON FEATURES BETWEEN OLD AND NEW STYLES. HERE, THE COLORS GOLD AND BLUE AND A STARBURST PATTERN IN THE WALLPAPER, ON THE DRESS FORM, AND ON THE SIDE OF THE CHAISE, UNIFY A ROOM OF UNIQUE AND DISPARATE OBJECTS.

WHEN FUSING STYLES, REPETITION AND CONTRAST ARE GOOD ALLIES. THE CIRCULAR SHAPE OF THESE UNUSUAL FORNASETTI DISHES PERCHED ABOVE THE DOORWAY FIND THEIR MATCH IN THE WAVY, CURVED DESIGN ON THE BACKSPLASH. AT THE SAME TIME, THE CHINA DISHES PROVIDE AN EFFECTIVE CONTRAST TO THE WOOD AND STEEL SURFACES.

color cues

Color is another easy to employ tactic for blending old and new. Nothing more than a simple, common color palette (especially white) can bring eclectic elements together beautifully. Another color trick is to tint white with the room's dominant hue and use it on trim throughout (for example, a room with ochre walls might benefit from a slight ochre tint to its white tint). The tint will subtly eliminate distraction and bring together the architecture of the space.

Floor color and texture can help unify the look from room to room: use the same material or finish through all the main rooms of the house, especially those with vistas into one another. Keep floor color neutral when possible, to act as a foil for the other colors in the room.

NOTICE THE SKILLFUL USE OF COLOR IN THESE ADJACENT ROOMS. THE SHARED GOLD AND GREEN ACCENTS, DARK WOOD TONES, AND BRIGHT WHITE TRIM CREATE A CONTINUOUS VISUAL FLOW FROM ONE ROOM TO THE NEXT.

YOU CAN MAINTAIN ALL THE CHARM OF AN EXISTING SPACE WITHOUT COMPROMISING YOUR MODERN AMBITIONS. ALLOW COOL, CONTEMPORARY ICE WHITE TO MERGE WITH AN ECLECTIC APPROACH TO STYLE, AS IN THIS BREAKFAST ROOM WITH ITS BEAUTIFUL COLLAGE OF FURNISHINGS AND SILHOUETTES. INTERESTING SHAPES ARE THE KEY HERE—THE LONG, NARROW BENCH, PAINTED TO MATCH THE POTTERY COLLECTION, LEADS YOUR GAZE TO THE CABINET. WHIMSY, TOO, IS EVIDENT IN THE MESH SCULPTURES, THE CURLY CURTAIN ROD, AND IN THE UNIQUE CHANDELIER.

natural materials

Natural materials, such as rattan, wicker, jute, linen, and cotton have a welcoming softness that can take the edge from bold combinations of old and new. Use the tactile allure of natural fabrics as a main element (at the windows, on the furniture, or as flooring,) to weave together objects you love taken from different periods and styles.

embellishment and serenity

When planning for change in a room, keep serenity at the top of your list. Too many accents or pieces of furniture will jar it away: too few will make the room seem barren. The simple tradition of pairing may help you decide what to keep in, what to edit, as you work on redefining a space. Pairing is the commonsense decorating technique of bringing furniture together: chairs placed side by side; a sofa with a coffee table; a settee with an ottoman, and so on. If each main piece of furniture is paired with its natural companion, the room layout will be full, but uncluttered, and the atmosphere will feel naturally serene.

If you've seen a Japanese or Asian-styled room, you have seen another trick of serenity at work: the height of individual furnishings does much to influence the atmosphere. If the majority of the furnishings are lower than 3 feet—the surface of the room appears very calm. In an eclectic mix, you can accomplish this by substituting large pillows for some of the room's seating, or (if you are in the market for a new piece of furniture) by choosing a bed, sofa, or coffee table that sits quite low to the ground. Especially in rooms where the treasure you wish to display is oversize (an armoire, a chest, or tansu, for example), this technique works beautifully. It has the added benefit of allowing many more small items to be displayed, without a sense of clutter.

QUIETLY MODERN AND LOUDLY ECLECTIC, HERE IS AN INTERIOR WHOSE SECRETS ARE IN THE DETAILS. PLAIN, CLEAN SISAL ON THE FLOOR AND A SWEEP OF BOLD COLOR ON THE WALLS LETS THE ECLECTIC ARRAY OF CHAIRS REIGN—THE CONTEMPORARY ARTWORK, SMALL MODERN LAMPS, AND UNDERSTATED FINISHES CONVEY A SENSE THAT THINGS MATCH IN A ROOM WHERE NOTHING DOES.

YOU CAN SUCCESSFULLY MIX ARTS AND CRAFTS WITH ATTIC HEIRLOOMS AND STILL GIVE A ROOM A MODERN AIR; THE KEY IS NOT TO HAVE TOO MANY OBJECTS IN THE ROOM. KEEP THE WINDOWS SIMPLE, THE WALLS PLAIN, AND INTRODUCE A MODERN ELEMENT OF SURPRISE. HERE, A COMB-PAINTED FLOOR JAZZES UP THE ROOM.

ON-LINE ANTIQUES AND TREASURES

In just one hour you can travel around the world and shop for antique furniture, handcrafts, posters, rugs, pottery, and ceramics, all of which is photographed well enough so you feel quite comfortable about making a purchase. The Internet lets you shop twenty-four hours a day 365 days a year in your desk chair. Now, you can sit home and explore a world you, perhaps, have always wondered about. For example, if you're wondering what Paris, Italy, or England has to offer in pine furniture, glass art, ceramics or vintage posters, you can be shopping in any of these countries seeing inventory. Here is a sampling of a few wonderful sites for armchair treasure hunting:

www.guild.com brings you the 1,300 artists via the Internet, with more than eight thousand art objects, and endorsements from the likes of *Time, Business Week,* and the *Wall Street Journal.*

www.artmecca.com offers art including ceramics, crafts, drawings, fiber and textiles, furniture, printmaking, sculptures, and jewelry. Like guild.com, their photography shows the art items clearly, and once you find something you like, you can read about the artist and see more of his or her work.

www.nextmonet.com is another user friendly site that prompts you to Artists of the Week, Highlights of Our Collection, their art-themed travel program, art advice, and learning about art. In addition to paintings, you can find affordable, hand-crafted home accessories, furniture and lighting, dining and entertaining items at this site.

www.internationalposter.com tells you everything you've ever wanted to know about collectable poster wall art, and shows many hundreds of wonderful posters.

www.bertimosaici.com is based in Scandicci, Italy. Here, you can explore the very unusual offerings of this artisan firm that produces art made from precious and semi-precious stones, an art form that dates to the 1500s. They specialize in tables, dressing tables, console tables and can also do custom work.

www.netshows.com/adorni is another Italian dealer (in Parma). They specialize in antique doors from the sixteenth to the twentieth century.

www.arca.net/arts_antiques/exhibition.htm is a veritable Yellow Pages of antiques resources.

www.barnantiques.com features everything from armoires to dining room tables, mirrors, art, antique fabrics, and small collectibles. This Web site is very easy to navigate, and very fast. They will also pack and ship items anywhere.

relaxed comfort

What is the recipe for the perfect eclectic room? Obviously, individual taste plays a starring role—but each of the rooms pictured in this chapter shares a sense of relaxed comfort: a simple, sophisticated approach that combines stylish looks with a few fundamental pleasures. If you use the modern elements in a room to celebrate objects with a past, the results will be comfortable and beautiful. How do you do this? Bring in color, use backdrops, and capitalize on the element of surprise.

perfect palettes

All white was once de rigeur for a truly Modern look, and it can still work well to suggest Modern in a room. However, if you give color a much bigger role to play on the walls, you will find surprising and beautiful results. Choose a warm, burnished hue-whether pale or saturated—and play it out over all the walls or just the largest visible surface. Persimmon, ochre, burgundy, Tuscan yellow, and warm, creamy hues make a room glow. Strong wall color, the interesting textures of treasured pieces, and pure white as an accent, make a strong formula for updated rooms that don't look stark.

SOMETIMES THE BEST DESIGN SOLUTIONS COME IN COMBINING INTERESTING SHAPES, DISREGARDING WHETHER THEIR UNION IS PRACTICAL. THE SWIRLS IN THE BURL OF THIS ANTIQUE CHEST WORK WELL WITH THE SOFT ROUNDNESS OF THE CONTEMPORARY POTTERY. ALSO EXPERIMENT WITH JUXTAPOSING LIGHT AND DARK OBJECTS, AND THROW IN A SURPRISE NOW AND THEN. THE BRIGHT RED REPTILE DOES JUST THAT—AND IT ECHOES THE SQUIGGLES OF THE MIRROR FRAME.

USE COLOR TO INTEGRATE OBJECTS TAKEN
FROM MANY STYLES AND PERIODS. IN THIS
ROOM, WALLS FLUSHED IN BRILLIANT
COLOR EMBRACE THE MEDLEY OF DISTINC-
TIVE ANTIQUES AND RETRO CHAIRS.

backdrops

Just as museums and galleries focus attention on art by setting against just the right background color, so can you take advantage of the "art of the backdrop." Lean a large modern piece against a mantel or fireplace trimmed in hand-painted tile. Let windows stand bare of all covering except shiny painted trim, and use them to highlight an ornate piece of furniture or other treasure. Bring color to a large wall in a room with lots of display, to provide a restful focal point.

SQUARE WALLS, FREE OF COLOR OR ARCHITECTURAL DETAILS, CAN PROVIDE GALLERY-LIKE SPACE FOR DISPLAYING A DIVERSE COLLECTION OF ART AND ANTIQUES. CONSIDER WORKING WITH A VERY SIMPLE PALETTE TO BEST SHOW-CASE THE COLLECTION.

YOU CAN CREATE THE IDEAL ECLECTIC
ZONE BY USING MINIMAL FURNISHINGS
AND WORKING THE VIEW WITH ANTIQUES
AND ARTWORK. THIS APPROACH WORKS
BEST IF YOU TAKE CARE TO KEEP THE
FLOORS AND WALLS PLAIN, AND KEEP
PATTERNED FABRICS OUT OF THE ROOM.

the element of surprise

Shake up a theme with visual surprise. Look around at your inventory. Is there a blank wall calling out for that big carved chest that's been hidden in another room? By making the chest a focal point and, perhaps, adding a modern sculpture to set on top of it, you will change the dynamics and energy in the room for the better.

Then again, there may be symmetry to be found by placing a pen-and-ink drawing and a wildly modern piece of art side by side. Search out surprising combinations such as these, and some very happy accidents will occur.

Remember, too, you can bring on the modern mood with art or furnishings that are very obviously from other cultures. You can satisfy a passion while you move in a whole new design direction.

Eclectic style enables the creative spirit, with the freedom to work in an informal, playful, and whimsical range. The easy elegance of pieces with a past, well-combined with a practical, modern approach to layout and flow are the essence of Modern Eclectic mixes, and the essence of rooms at their best.

YOU CAN EASILY SHOWCASE A LARGE ANTIQUE AND STILL KEEP THE MOOD CONTEMPORARY. BALANCE THE ROOM BY GROUPING OLD AND NEW OBJECTS SEPARATELY. OLD-FASHIONED ACCESSORIES REST EASILY ON THIS ANTIQUE SIDEBOARD, WHICH GOES NICELY WITH THE CHOCOLATE-HUED WALLS, BRIGHT WHITE MOLDINGS, AND TRIM DINING SET. NOTICE, TOO, HOW THE MODERN ACCENTS DRAW ATTENTION TO THE CENTER OF THIS ECLECTIC SPACE.

MIX SLEEK, MODERN CABINETRY WITH
PRECIOUS COLLECTIONS TO ADD COLOR,
DIMENSION, AND INTERESTING SHAPES
TO A SIMPLE DESIGN. THE PASTEL POT-
TERY IN A VARIETY OF SHAPES AND SIZES
FUSES NICELY WITH THE MUTED HUES IN
THIS CONTEMPORARY KITCHEN. NOTICE
HOW THE SHELVING IS CUED SUBTLY
FROM THE PAST.

photo credits

Antoine Bootz, 101; 109
Tim Clinch/The Interior Archive, 55
Courtesy of California Closets, 52
Grey Crawford/Beateworks, 34; 37; 42; 53; 60; 79
Christopher Drake/Red Cover, 15 (bottom); 17; 39; 58; 71; 76; 85; 135
Brian Harrison/Red Cover, 86; 89
Ken Hayden/Red Cover, 23; 24; 25; 40; 62; 68; 77; 97 (top); 122; 129
Winfried Heinze/Red Cover, 16 (left); 38; 43; 67; 93; 95 (bottom)
Anna Kasabian, 21; 98
Keller & Keller, 112, 113; 125
Neil Lorimer/Elizabeth Whiting Assocs., 12
Courtesy of Herman Miller, 78
Eric Roth, 5; 20 (both); 81; 82; 83; 87; 95 (top); 105; 110; 111; 114; 115; 116; 117;
    119 (both); 120; 123; 126; 127; 131; 133; 136
Eric Roth/Charles Spada Interiors,104
Jeremy Samuelson, 41
Kim Sayer/Red Cover, 59 (top)
Tim Street-Porter/Beateworks, 44; 49
Andrew Twort/Red Cover, 69
Simon Upton/The Interior Archive, 72; 73; 74 (left); 97 (bottom); 124
Brian Vanden Brink, 9; 11; 13; 18; 19; 46; 48 (both); 54
Brian Vanden Brink/ Elliott & Elliott Architects, 103
Brian Vanden Brink/Thom Rouselle, Architect, 99
Edina van der Wyck/The Interior Archive, 56; 107
Fritz von der Schulenburg/The Interior Archive, 59 (bottom); 61; 65
Andreas von Einsiedel/Red Cover, 14; 16 (right); 22; 26; 27; 28; 29; 30; 31; 33; 35;
    36; 45; 51; 63; 64; 66; 70; 74 (right); 75; 91 (both); 106; 121; 133
Dominique Vorillon/Beateworks, 47
Elizabeth Whiting Assocs., 15 (top)
Andrew Wood/The Interior Archive, 57

acknowledgments

I would like to thank Shawna Mullen, my editor for giving me yet another wonderful project, and a design theme (mixing periods) that I not only believe in but live. Special thanks to photo editor Betsy Gammons for gathering all the beautiful pictures. And special thank-yous to Gayle Mandle, Ann & Chris Fitzgerald, and Chef Lydia Shire for sharing your wonderful homes in these pages.

—AK

Thanks to Shawna, who encouraged me to stretch from bricks and mortar to fabrics and finishes. To Jay, Kristy, and Robert, who kept me in good humor.

—NRG

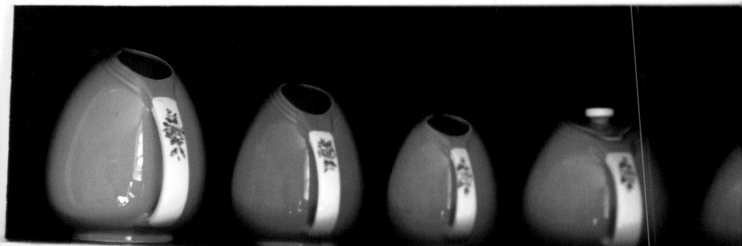

dedication

This book is dedicated to my Aunt Lena whose home and children gave me a history of laughter and fun and whose spirit lives in me. Neither of us follow the rules.

—AK

...to those readers who embrace the challenge and spirit of Modern Nostalgia. And, as always, with love to William.

—NRG

about the authors

Anna Kasabian is the author of *Designing Interiors with Tile: Creative Ideas with Ceramics, Stone, and Mosaic, East Coast Rooms, The New Home Color Book,* and *Kids' Rooms: A Hands-On Decorating Guide.* She is also a contributor to *Cooking Spaces* (all by Rockport Publishers). Her byline frequently appears in the *Boston Globe, Woman's Day, Boston* magazine, and *New England Travel and Life.* She scouts and produces for HGTV and has appeared on various home design segments as well.

Nora Richter Greer is a freelance author/editor who has written about architecture and design for more than twenty years. Her career began at *Architecture* magazine. She is the author or coauthor of nine books, including *Architecture Transformed, Architecture as Response, The Right Light, Design Secrets: Architectural Interiors* (all by Rockport Publishers), *Hot Dirt, Cool Straw* (Hearst Publication) and *The Search for Shelter* (AIA Press).